HOW TO HELP
YOUR WIFE HEAL
FROM YOUR
AFFAIR

"Rebuilding trust is not sprint, it's a marathon"

Steve Collins

Healing from affairs 2

Contents

Introduction

Once upon a time, my sister, Anabel, came to me for help after discovering that her husband had been unfaithful to her. As a trained relationship counselor, I knew exactly what to do to help her heal and move forward.

The first thing we did was establish trust and confidentiality in our relationship. She needed to feel safe and comfortable sharing her feelings and experiences with me, so I made sure to provide her with a non-judgmental and supportive environment.

We began by talking about the different emotions she was experiencing, such as anger, hurt, and betrayal. I encouraged her to express her feelings and validated her emotions, letting her know that what she was going through was completely normal.

Together, we worked on developing a plan to help her move forward. We talked about setting boundaries with her husband, such as not accepting any lies or deceit, and we discussed ways to communicate more effectively.

I also helped her to recognize that her husband's infidelity was not her fault and that it was not a reflection of her worth as a person. This was an important realization for her, and it helped her to start rebuilding her self-esteem and confidence.

Through our counseling sessions, Anabel began to heal from the pain of her husband's infidelity. She was able to forgive him, not because he deserved it, but because she knew that holding onto anger and resentment would only hurt herself.

In the end, Anabel and her husband were able to work through their issues and rebuild their relationship on a foundation of honesty, trust, and love. I was proud to have been able to help my sister through such a difficult time and to see her emerge stronger and more resilient as a result. In this book, we are going to reveal all the secrets we deployed to help Anabel heal from the affairs of her husband. This secret has also helped hundreds of other people to rebuild their relationships.

Infidelity is one of the most devastating and heartbreaking experiences that a couple can go through. The betrayal, lies, and deceit can shatter the foundation of a marriage, leaving both parties feeling lost, hurt, and unsure of how to move forward.

If you're reading this, you've likely made the painful choice to cheat on your spouse and are now grappling with the consequences of your actions. But it's important to acknowledge that there is hope for your relationship, and you can work towards rebuilding the trust and love that may have been lost.

This book, "How to Help Your Wife Heal from Your Affair," is a comprehensive guide that will provide you with the tools and strategies you need to support your spouse as she navigates the complex emotions and challenges that come with healing from infidelity.

Drawing on the latest research in psychology and personal experience, this book offers practical advice and step-by-step guidance for husbands who want to make amends and help their wives recover from the trauma of betrayal.

Whether you've just revealed your affair, or you've been working on rebuilding your relationship for some time, this book will give you a clear roadmap for moving forward. From understanding your wife's perspective to building a strong support system, each chapter offers actionable advice that will help you and your spouse heal and grow together.

But this book isn't just for men who have cheated. It's also for women who are struggling to come to terms with their partner's infidelity. If you're a wife who has been betrayed, this book will offer you valuable insight into your spouse's perspective, as well as tips for managing your own emotions and moving towards forgiveness.

Infidelity can be an incredibly painful experience for everyone involved, but it doesn't have to mean the end of your marriage. With dedication, commitment, and a willingness to work through the challenges, you and your spouse can emerge from this crisis with a stronger, more loving relationship than ever before.

So if you're ready to take the first step towards healing and rebuilding your relationship, then this book is for you. Let's work together to create a brighter future for you and your spouse.

Chapter One

The Reality of Infidelity

Defining Infidelity and its Impact on Relationships

Infidelity refers to the act of engaging in a romantic or sexual relationship with someone other than one's partner, while still in a committed relationship. Infidelity can have a significant impact on relationships and can lead to emotional distress, mistrust, and even the breakdown of the relationship. Here are some ways that infidelity can impact relationships:

Trust issues: Infidelity can shatter trust in a relationship, and trust is a foundation of a healthy relationship. When someone cheats, it breaks the trust that has been built up over time, and it can be challenging to rebuild it. The betrayed partner may find it difficult to trust their partner again, even if they apologize and promise to never do it again.

Emotional distress: Infidelity can cause significant emotional distress, leading to feelings of anger, sadness, depression, and anxiety. The betrayed partner may experience feelings of betrayal, humiliation, and rejection, which can cause long-lasting emotional damage.

Communication breakdown: Infidelity can also lead to a breakdown in communication between partners. The betrayed partner may struggle to express their feelings, and the cheating partner may avoid talking about the infidelity, leading to a breakdown in communication.

Physical health consequences: Infidelity can also lead to physical health consequences, such as sexually transmitted infections (STIs) or unwanted pregnancies, which can further complicate the situation and put the health of both partners at risk.

Guilt and shame: Infidelity can also lead to feelings of guilt and shame for both the betrayed and cheating partners. The cheating partner may feel guilty for their actions, while the betrayed partner may feel ashamed for not being enough for their partner.

Difficulty in moving forward: Infidelity can also make it challenging for the couple to move forward in their relationship. It can be difficult to rebuild trust, and the betrayed partner may struggle to forgive their partner and move on.

The aftermath of infidelity for both partners

Infidelity can have a profound impact on both partners involved in the relationship. The aftermath of infidelity can be a difficult and complex experience that requires time, effort, and patience from both individuals to work through.

For the partner who has been cheated on, the aftermath of infidelity can be emotionally devastating. They may experience a range of emotions such as shock, anger, sadness, betrayal, and loss of trust. It is common for them to struggle with feelings of self-doubt, questioning whether they are worthy of love and respect. The betrayed partner may also experience physical symptoms, such as difficulty sleeping, appetite changes, and anxiety.

For the partner who cheated, the aftermath of infidelity can be equally challenging. They may experience guilt, shame, and remorse for their actions. It is common for them to feel overwhelmed and unsure of how to make amends for their behavior. They may struggle with issues of self-esteem and self-worth, as well as fear of rejection or abandonment.

Both partners may benefit from seeking professional help, such as individual or couples counseling. Counseling can provide a safe and supportive space for each partner to process their emotions, communicate their needs and concerns, and work toward rebuilding trust and intimacy.

In order to move forward after infidelity, both partners need to take responsibility for their actions and be willing to work together to repair the damage caused by the betrayal. This may involve setting new boundaries, improving communication, and practicing forgiveness. It is important for each partner to be patient and compassionate with one another, as healing from infidelity is a process that takes time and effort.

Understanding the complex emotions involved

Infidelity can be an emotionally complex experience for both partners involved in a relationship. Understanding the various emotions that may arise can be key to processing and moving through the aftermath of infidelity.

For the partner who has been cheated on, emotions such as shock, anger, sadness, and betrayal are common. These emotions can be overwhelming and may manifest in physical symptoms, such as difficulty sleeping, changes in appetite, and anxiety. The betrayed partner may also experience a loss of trust and a sense of insecurity in the relationship, as well as self-doubt and questioning of their self-worth.

For the partner who cheated, emotions such as guilt, shame, and remorse are common. They may also experience fear of rejection or abandonment, as well as uncertainty about how to make amends for their behavior. The cheater may struggle with issues of self-esteem and self-worth and may require support to address underlying issues that contributed to the infidelity.

It is important for both partners to recognize and validate each other's emotions, and to avoid judgment or criticism. Each person's experience is unique, and processing emotions may take time and patience. It may be helpful to seek professional help, such as individual or couples counseling, to work through complex emotions and communication challenges.

Communication is also key to understanding the complex emotions involved in infidelity. Each partner should have the opportunity to express their feelings and needs and listen actively to their partner's perspective. This can help to build empathy and compassion and foster a sense of mutual understanding and respect.

The Road to Healing and rebuilding trust

The road to healing and rebuilding trust after infidelity can be a long and difficult process, but it is possible with time, effort, and commitment from both partners. Here are some key steps to consider when working towards rebuilding trust:

Take responsibility for your actions: The partner who cheated must take full responsibility for their actions and express sincere remorse for the hurt they have caused. This may involve apologizing, making amends, and showing a willingness to work on repairing the relationship.

Be patient and understanding: Healing from infidelity can take time, and it is important for both partners to be patient and understanding with each other. Avoid putting pressure on the healing process, and allow each other the space and time needed to work through emotions and build trust.

Communicate openly and honestly: Communication is key to rebuilding trust. Both partners should be open and honest about their feelings, needs, and concerns, and should listen actively to each other's perspective. Avoid blame, criticism, and defensiveness, and strive to communicate in a way that fosters empathy and understanding.

Set clear boundaries: Rebuilding trust often requires setting clear boundaries and expectations for behavior moving forward. Both partners should have the opportunity to express what they need in order to feel safe and secure in the relationship and should work together to establish guidelines for behavior.

Seek professional help if needed: Infidelity can be a complex and emotionally challenging experience, and it may be helpful to seek professional help to navigate the healing process. Consider couples counseling, individual therapy, or support groups as a means of getting the support and guidance needed to rebuild trust.

Rebuilding trust after infidelity is not easy, but with commitment, patience, and a willingness to work together, it is possible to repair the damage caused by betrayal and create a stronger, more resilient relationship.

Chapter Two

Taking Responsibility for Your Affair

Acknowledging the pain and hurt caused by the affair

Acknowledging the pain and hurt caused by the affair is an important step toward healing and rebuilding trust in a relationship. It can be difficult to face the hurt that has been caused, but it is necessary in order to move forward and begin the healing process.

Here are some ways to acknowledge the pain and hurt caused by the affair:

Take responsibility for your actions: If you were the partner who cheated, it is important to take responsibility for your actions and acknowledge the hurt that you have caused. This may involve apologizing, expressing sincere remorse, and being open and honest about your motivations and behaviors.

Listen actively: It is important to listen actively to your partner's perspective and acknowledge the pain and hurt that they are experiencing. Avoid being defensive or dismissive, and instead, listen with empathy and a willingness to understand their point of view.

Validate feelings: It is important to validate your partner's feelings of hurt, anger, and betrayal. Let them know that you understand how much pain they are experiencing and that you are committed to doing what it takes to repair the damage that has been done.

Avoid minimizing the hurt: It is important to avoid minimizing the hurt caused by the affair. Even if you believe that your actions were not intended to cause harm, it is important to acknowledge the impact that they had on your partner and take steps to repair the damage.

Be patient: Healing from infidelity can take time, and it is important to be patient with the process. Recognize that your partner may need time and space to work through their emotions, and be willing to provide the support and understanding that they need.

Acknowledging the pain and hurt caused by the affair is an important step toward healing and rebuilding trust in a relationship. It requires honesty, empathy, and a willingness to take responsibility for your actions and repair the damage that has been done. With commitment and effort from both partners, it is possible to move forward and create a stronger, more resilient relationship.

The importance of taking responsibility for your actions

Taking responsibility for your actions after infidelity is crucial for rebuilding trust and repairing the damage caused by the affair. Here are some reasons why taking responsibility is so important in this context:

It demonstrates accountability: When you take responsibility for your actions after infidelity, you demonstrate accountability and a willingness to own your mistakes. This can help to rebuild trust and create a sense of safety and security in the relationship.

It shows empathy: Taking responsibility for your actions after infidelity involves showing empathy and understanding for your partner's pain and hurt. By acknowledging the impact of your actions and taking steps to repair the damage, you can demonstrate that you care about your partner's feelings and are committed to making things right.

It promotes healing: Taking responsibility for your actions can help to promote healing and create a sense of closure for both partners. By owning up to your mistakes and making a sincere effort to repair the damage, you can create a foundation for moving forward and rebuilding a stronger, more resilient relationship.

It builds trust: Taking responsibility for your actions after infidelity is a key component of rebuilding trust. By demonstrating accountability and a willingness to make things right, you can help your partner feel more secure and confident in the relationship.

It sets a positive example: Taking responsibility for your actions after infidelity can set a positive example for others to follow. By demonstrating accountability and integrity, you can inspire those around you to take ownership of their mistakes and work to repair any damage that they have caused.

Understanding the reasons behind the affair

Understanding the reasons behind an affair is an important part of healing and moving forward after infidelity. It can provide insight into the underlying issues that contributed to the affair and help both partners work to address those issues in order to strengthen the relationship. Here are some important points to consider when trying to understand the reasons behind an affair:

There is no single cause: Affairs can be complex and have many different causes. Some common factors that may contribute to an affair include issues with intimacy, unmet emotional needs, lack of communication, unresolved conflicts, and personal insecurities. It is important to understand that there is no single cause for an affair, and it is often the result of a combination of factors.

It is not always about the partner: While an affair can be devastating to the partner, it is important to understand that it is not always about them. Many times, the reasons behind the affair are more about the person who had the affair and their own emotional and psychological needs. This does not excuse the behavior, but it can help to put it into context and make it easier to understand.

It requires open communication: In order to understand the reasons behind an affair, both partners need to be willing to engage in open and honest communication. This can be difficult, as it requires vulnerability and a willingness to confront difficult emotions and issues. However, it is essential for both partners to be able to express their feelings and concerns in a safe and non-judgmental environment.

It can be a process: Understanding the reasons behind an affair is often a process that takes time and effort. It may require the help of a therapist or counselor, as well as a willingness on the part of both partners to explore their own emotions and behaviors in order to gain a deeper understanding of what led to the affair.

It can lead to growth and healing: While confronting the reasons behind an affair can be painful, it can also lead to growth and healing for both partners. By addressing underlying issues and working to build a stronger, more resilient relationship, both partners can emerge from the experience with a deeper understanding of themselves and each other.

Taking ownership of your actions

Taking ownership of your actions is especially important after affairs, as infidelity can have significant emotional and psychological consequences for both partners. Here are some important points to consider when taking ownership of your actions after an affair:

Acknowledge the impact of your actions: It's important to acknowledge the hurt and pain caused by your actions and the impact they have had on your partner. This can involve taking responsibility for the breach of trust, acknowledging the emotional harm caused, and expressing remorse and empathy for the pain your partner is experiencing.

Identify the reasons behind the affair: Taking ownership of your actions also involves understanding the reasons behind the affair. This may involve exploring issues related to intimacy, communication, unresolved conflicts, personal insecurities, and other factors that may have contributed to the breach of trust.

Accept accountability: Accepting accountability means taking responsibility for your actions and being willing to face the consequences. This may involve making changes in your behavior, such as being more transparent, increasing communication, or seeking professional help to address underlying issues.

Show a willingness to make amends: Taking ownership of your actions also involves showing a willingness to make amends and working towards rebuilding trust. This may involve apologizing to your partner, being transparent and open about your actions, and making efforts to rebuild emotional intimacy and connection.

Maintain a commitment to growth and change: Taking ownership of your actions after an affair also involves maintaining a commitment to growth and change. This may involve seeking counseling or therapy to address underlying issues, practicing better communication and conflict resolution skills, and making a conscious effort to rebuild trust and emotional intimacy in the relationship.

Rebuilding trust through action

Rebuilding trust after an affair is a long and difficult process, but it is possible with patience, commitment, and consistent action. Here are some ways to rebuild trust through action after your affairs:

Be honest and transparent: To rebuild trust, it is crucial to prioritize honesty and transparency. This involves being candid with your partner about your thoughts, feelings, and actions. It also means being open with your communication and keeping your partner informed of your whereabouts and activities. By prioritizing honesty and transparency, you can work towards creating a strong foundation of trust in your relationship.

Ensure to honor your commitments: Only promise what you can deliver, and make sure to follow through on those promises. If you pledge to modify a specific behavior, ensure that you remain consistent and dedicated to fulfilling that promise.

Be consistent in your behavior: Consistency is key to rebuilding trust. Make sure that your actions and words align with your commitment to rebuilding trust. Demonstrate your commitment to your partner through your consistent behavior.

Respect your partner's feelings: Be respectful of your partner's feelings, concerns, and boundaries. Show that you understand the impact of your actions and are willing to make changes to help rebuild the relationship.

Seek counseling or therapy: Consider seeking counseling or therapy to work through the emotional trauma of infidelity and to learn better communication and conflict resolution skills. A trained therapist can help you and your partner work through your feelings, understand each other's perspectives, and develop a plan for rebuilding trust.

Be patient: Time and patience are crucial in this process, which cannot be hurried or coerced. Give your partner the necessary time to deal with their emotions and engage in trust-building behaviors, and remain patient as you both strive to rebuild trust.

Be accountable: Take full responsibility for your actions and be accountable for the consequences. Show that you are willing to make things right and work towards rebuilding trust.

Demonstrate your love and commitment:
Show your partner that you love them and are committed to rebuilding the relationship. This can be done through actions such as planning special dates, expressing affection, and consistently showing your partner that they are a priority in your life.

Healing from affairs 36

Chapter Three

Supporting Your Wife's Healing Process

Creating a safe and supportive environment for your wife

Creating a safe and supportive environment for your wife after your affairs is crucial in helping her heal and rebuild trust in the relationship. Here are some ways to create a safe and supportive environment for your wife:

Be empathetic: Put yourself in your wife's shoes and try to understand how she feels. Show her that you care about her feelings and are willing to work with her to rebuild the relationship.

Communicate effectively: Communication is key in any relationship, especially when trying to rebuild trust after infidelity. Be open and honest with your wife, and listen actively to her concerns and needs.

Avoid defensiveness: When discussing the affair, avoid becoming defensive or trying to justify your actions. This can make your wife feel like her feelings and concerns are being dismissed.

Respect your wife's boundaries: Be respectful of your wife's boundaries and needs. If she needs time alone or space, give it to her.

Take responsibility for your actions: Take full responsibility for your actions and show your wife that you are willing to make amends and work towards rebuilding trust.

Be patient: Healing and rebuilding trust take time. Be patient and understanding with your wife, and don't rush her healing process.

Be supportive: Show your wife that you are there for her and support her emotionally. This can be done through gestures such as listening to her, offering a shoulder to cry on, or helping her with daily tasks.

Show appreciation: Show your wife that you appreciate her and value her. This can be done through small gestures such as sending a thoughtful text, writing a letter expressing your gratitude, or planning a special date.

Seek counseling or therapy: Consider seeking counseling or therapy to help you and your wife work through the emotional trauma of infidelity and learn better communication and conflict-resolution skills.

Active listening and empathizing with your wife's feelings

Active listening and empathizing with your wife's feelings are critical components of rebuilding trust and healing after infidelity. Here are some ways to practice active listening and empathizing with your wife's feelings:

Pay attention: When your wife is speaking, give her your undivided attention. Put away your phone, turn off the TV, and make eye contact with her. This shows her that you value and respect her.

Listen attentively without interruption: It is important to refrain from interrupting your wife while she is speaking, even if you hold a different perspective. It is crucial to allow her to express her thoughts completely before responding.

Acknowledge her feelings: It is essential to recognize and acknowledge your wife's emotions, even if you do not share the same perspective. Communicate to her that you understand her sentiments and that her feelings are legitimate.

Reflect back: Repeat back to your wife what you heard her say, using your own words. This helps to clarify any misunderstandings and shows your wife that you are truly listening.

Pose open-ended inquiries: Use open-ended questions to encourage your wife to express more about her emotions and experiences. Steer clear of questions that can be responded to with a simple "yes" or "no".

Practice empathy: Put yourself in your wife's shoes and try to understand how she feels. Empathy involves acknowledging and sharing her emotions, even if you haven't experienced them herself.

Avoid defensiveness: When listening to your wife's feelings and concerns, avoid becoming defensive or trying to justify your actions. This can make your wife feel like her feelings and concerns are being dismissed.

Show understanding: Show your wife that you understand how difficult this situation is for her and that you are committed to working through it together.

By actively listening and empathizing with your wife's feelings, you can help her feel heard and understood. This can lead to greater trust and emotional intimacy in your relationship. Remember to validate her feelings, reflect back on what you heard, and avoid becoming defensive. With time and effort, you can rebuild trust and heal together after infidelity.

Encouraging open and honest communication

Encouraging open and honest communication is crucial to rebuilding trust and healing after infidelity. Here are some ways to foster open and honest communication in your relationship:

Create a safe space: Make sure your wife feels safe to express her thoughts and emotions without fear of judgment or retaliation. This requires creating an environment that is free from blame, criticism, and defensiveness.

Practice active listening: Actively listen to your wife when she speaks. Show genuine interest in what she is saying and avoid interrupting her. Reflect back on what you heard to ensure you understand her perspective.

Be honest and transparent: Take responsibility for your actions and be honest with your wife about what happened. Avoid hiding details or downplaying the affair.

Ask for feedback: Ask your wife for feedback on how you can support her in the healing process. Encourage her to share her thoughts, feelings, and concerns, and show a willingness to address them.

Validate your wife's feelings: Validate your wife's emotions and let her know that you understand why she feels the way she does. This shows her that you are listening and that her feelings matter.

Avoid becoming defensive: Avoid becoming defensive when your wife shares her thoughts and feelings with you. Instead, try to understand where she is coming from and respond with empathy.

Set boundaries: Set clear boundaries around communication. Agree on how often you will talk about the affair and what topics are off-limits. This can help both of you feel more comfortable and secure.

Consider seeking professional assistance: It may be helpful to consult a therapist or counselor, who can offer guidance and support as you navigate the process of rebuilding trust and healing after experiencing infidelity. A trained professional can provide valuable insights and assistance to aid you in overcoming the challenges.

By encouraging open and honest communication, you can create a foundation for rebuilding trust and strengthening your relationship. Remember to create a safe space, practice active listening, be honest and transparent, and validate your wife's feelings. With time, effort, and a commitment to communication, you can heal together and move forward as a stronger couple.

Chapter Four

Understanding Your Wife's Perspective

The emotional impact of Infidelity on Women

Infidelity can have a significant emotional impact on women, causing feelings of hurt, betrayal, and insecurity. Here are some of the emotional effects that infidelity can have on women:

Loss of trust: One of the most significant emotional impacts of infidelity on women is the loss of trust. Women may feel that they can no longer trust their partner or anyone else in their life. The betrayal of infidelity can shatter the foundation of trust that a relationship is built on.

The feeling of rejection: Infidelity can leave women feeling rejected and unworthy of love. They may blame themselves for their partner's infidelity, even though it is not their fault.

Anger: Women may experience intense anger towards their partner for the pain and betrayal caused by the infidelity. They may feel a sense of rage and desire for revenge.

Grief: Infidelity can also cause a sense of grief and loss for the relationship that once was. Women may mourn the loss of the trust, intimacy, and emotional connection they once shared with their partner.

Shame and embarrassment: Women may feel shame and embarrassment about the infidelity, even though they did nothing wrong. They may feel like they have failed in their relationship and fear judgment from others.

Anxiety and depression: Infidelity can lead to feelings of anxiety, depression, and other mental health issues. Women may experience a loss of appetite, difficulty sleeping, and a lack of motivation.

Low self-esteem: Infidelity can cause women to question their worth and value. They may feel inadequate and unlovable, leading to a decline in self-esteem.

It is important to note that the emotional impact of infidelity can vary from woman to woman, and some may not experience all of these emotions. However, it is critical to acknowledge and validate the emotional pain and trauma that infidelity can cause. Seeking professional help from a therapist or counselor can be beneficial in processing and healing from the emotional impact of infidelity.

Empathy and understanding your wife's emotions

Empathy and understanding are essential components in helping your wife heal from the emotional trauma caused by your infidelity. Here are some ways in which you can demonstrate empathy and understanding toward your wife's emotions:

Acknowledge her pain: It is essential to validate your wife's feelings and acknowledge the pain and hurt caused by your infidelity. Show empathy by expressing regret and apologizing for the pain you have caused.

Listen actively: Listening actively involves giving your full attention to your wife when she is expressing her emotions. Pay attention to her tone, body language, and words to understand her feelings. Avoid interrupting her or getting defensive when she is sharing her emotions.

Put yourself in her shoes: Try to imagine how your wife is feeling and how you would feel in her situation. This helps you understand her perspective and empathize with her emotions.

Show compassion: Compassion involves being kind, caring, and understanding toward your wife's emotional state. Show her that you care by offering comfort, support, and reassurance.

Take responsibility: Taking responsibility for your actions is a crucial step in showing empathy towards your wife. Accept accountability for your mistakes and be willing to make amends to help your wife heal.

Be patient: Healing from infidelity takes time, and it is essential to be patient with your wife as she processes her emotions. Avoid pressuring her to forgive or move on quickly, and instead, focus on creating a safe and supportive environment for her.

By demonstrating empathy and understanding toward your wife's emotions, you can help her feel heard, validated, and supported. This, in turn, can help rebuild trust and strengthen your relationship. Remember that healing from infidelity is a process, and it takes time, effort, and commitment from both partners.

The importance of validating your wife's experience

Validating your wife's experience is an important aspect of helping her heal from the emotional trauma caused by your infidelity. Here are some reasons why validating her experience is important:

Helps her feel heard and understood: When you validate your wife's experience, you show her that you are listening and that her emotions are important to you. This can help her feel heard and understood, which is essential for healing.

Builds trust: Validating your wife's experience can help rebuild trust in your relationship. When you acknowledge the pain and hurt caused by your infidelity, you demonstrate your willingness to take responsibility for your actions and to work towards rebuilding the relationship.

Improves communication: Validating your wife's experience can improve communication between you and your wife. When you listen actively and respond empathetically, you create a safe space for open and honest communication. This can help improve the quality of your conversations and strengthen your relationship.

Increases emotional intimacy: Validating your wife's experience can increase emotional intimacy between you and your wife. When you show empathy and understanding toward her emotions, you create a deeper connection and a greater sense of intimacy.

Supports her healing process: Validating your wife's experience is an important step in supporting her healing process. It can help her process her emotions and move toward forgiveness and healing.

Chapter Five

Coping with the Aftermath

Understanding the emotional rollercoaster of healing

Healing from the emotional trauma of infidelity can be a rollercoaster of emotions for both partners. Here are some key points to understand about the emotional rollercoaster of healing:

It's a process: Healing from infidelity is not a linear process. It involves ups and downs, setbacks, and progress. Understanding that healing is a process and that it takes time can help you manage your expectations and remain patient throughout the journey.

There are many emotions involved: Healing from infidelity can involve a wide range of emotions, including anger, sadness, confusion, guilt, shame, and fear. It's important to recognize that these emotions are all normal and valid and to allow yourself and your partner to feel and express them.

Emotions can be intense: The emotions involved in healing from infidelity can be intense and overwhelming at times. It's important to find healthy ways to cope with these emotions, such as through therapy, exercise, or talking to a trusted friend.

Trust can be fragile: Rebuilding trust after infidelity is a delicate process. It takes time, effort, and consistent behavior on the part of the partner who was unfaithful. It's important to be patient and to recognize that trust may take longer to rebuild than you expect.

Communication is key: Effective communication is essential for healing from infidelity. It's important to be open and honest with each other about your feelings and to actively listen to each other's perspectives. This can help build empathy, understanding, and trust.

Forgiveness is a process: Forgiveness is a process, not an event. It takes time and effort to reach a place of forgiveness, and it's important to recognize that forgiveness may not happen overnight. It's also important to note that forgiveness does not mean forgetting or condoning the infidelity, but rather choosing to let go of the anger and resentment associated with it.

Self-care is important: Healing from infidelity can be emotionally draining, so it's important to prioritize self-care throughout the process. This can include taking time for yourself, engaging in activities that bring you joy, and seeking support from friends, family, or a therapist.

Coping strategies for both partners

Infidelity can have a significant impact on both partners in a relationship. It can cause a range of emotions, from anger and betrayal to confusion and sadness. Coping with these emotions can be challenging, but it's essential for both partners to find healthy ways to cope with the aftermath of infidelity. Here are some coping strategies for both partners:

Seek support: Both partners can benefit from seeking support from a therapist, counselor, or support group. This can provide a safe space to express feelings and receive guidance on coping with the aftermath of infidelity.

Practice self-care: It is important for both partners to focus on their physical and emotional health by practicing self-care. This may involve getting adequate sleep, maintaining a balanced diet, and engaging in activities that promote relaxation and happiness.

Communicate openly: Both partners should practice open and honest communication to build trust and understand each other's needs and feelings.

Set boundaries: Both partners may need to set boundaries to protect themselves from further emotional harm. This may involve limiting contact with the outside party or taking a break from the relationship to heal.

Practice forgiveness: Forgiveness can be a powerful tool for healing, but it's a process that takes time. Both partners should work towards forgiveness and focus on the present rather than dwelling on the past.

Focus on the positive: Both partners can benefit from focusing on the positive aspects of their relationship and celebrating their strengths. This can help build a foundation for healing and moving forward.

Take responsibility: Both partners should take responsibility for their actions and work towards making positive changes in themselves and their relationship.

Coping with the aftermath of infidelity can be a challenging process, but with the right support and strategies, both partners can heal and move forward toward a healthier and happier relationship.

Navigating difficult conversations and triggers

Navigating difficult conversations and triggers is an essential aspect of healing and rebuilding a relationship after infidelity. Here are some strategies for navigating difficult conversations and triggers:

Establish a safe space: Both partners should agree on a time and place to have the conversation, where they feel comfortable and safe to express their thoughts and feelings.

Use "I" statements: When discussing sensitive topics, use "I" statements to express your feelings and experiences, rather than accusing or blaming the other person. This can help avoid defensiveness and promote understanding.

Practice active listening: Both partners should practice active listening, which involves fully concentrating on what the other person is saying and repeating back what you hear to ensure understanding.

Take breaks: If the conversation becomes too overwhelming, both partners should agree on taking breaks to cool down and regroup before continuing the discussion.

Identify triggers: Both partners should identify triggers that cause negative emotions and avoid them whenever possible. This may include avoiding certain topics or situations.

Work on coping skills: Both partners should work on developing coping skills to manage triggers when they arise. This may include deep breathing, mindfulness, or talking to a trusted friend or therapist.

Seek professional help: If the conversation becomes too difficult to manage, both partners should consider seeking the help of a professional therapist or counselor to mediate and guide the conversation.

Navigating difficult conversations and triggers can be challenging, but with practice, patience, and understanding, both partners can work toward healing and rebuilding a stronger relationship. It's essential to remember that healing takes time and requires commitment from both partners.

Chapter Six

Rebuilding Trust

The importance of trust in your relationship

In any relationship, trust is an indispensable foundation. It is the confidence and assurance that your partner is truthful, dependable, and loyal. There are several reasons why trust is a crucial element in a relationship:

Trust promotes security: When you trust your partner, you feel secure in the relationship, which allows you to be vulnerable and open with them. This fosters intimacy and closeness.

Trust promotes communication: When there is trust in a relationship, it promotes open and honest communication. You feel safe to express your thoughts and feelings without fear of judgment or rejection.

Trust fosters respect: Trusting your partner shows that you respect them and their choices. This mutual respect helps to create a positive and healthy dynamic in the relationship.

Trust builds commitment: When you trust your partner, you are more likely to commit to the relationship long-term. This commitment strengthens the bond between partners.

Trust helps to manage conflict: When there is trust in a relationship, it helps to manage conflict more effectively. You can trust that your partner has your best interests at heart and will work with you to find a resolution.

Trust is essential for emotional and physical intimacy: Trust is a crucial ingredient for building emotional and physical intimacy in a relationship. It allows you to feel safe and secure with your partner, which enhances your connection.

Trust promotes personal growth: Trusting your partner allows you to grow as an individual and as a couple. It creates a safe space to explore your hopes, fears, and aspirations.

Rebuilding trust through transparency and accountability

Infidelity can cause severe damage to the trust between partners, making it difficult to rebuild the relationship. One way to start rebuilding trust is through transparency and accountability. Here are some ways to do that:

Open communication: Communication is key when rebuilding trust. Being open and honest with your partner about your actions, feelings, and intentions can help to create a foundation of trust. Share your thoughts, emotions, and reasons behind the infidelity, but also listen actively to your partner's perspective.

Consistency: Consistency is crucial when rebuilding trust. It's essential to follow through on your commitments and promises to your partner.

Show up when you say you will, and be reliable in all aspects of the relationship.

Transparency: Transparency in a relationship implies the willingness to disclose information regarding your actions and decisions to your partner. This involves being candid and truthful about your location, the company you keep, and your activities. It also means being receptive to any queries your partner might have.

Accountability: Taking responsibility for your actions and being accountable for your mistakes is another essential aspect of rebuilding trust. It means owning up to your mistakes, apologizing, and making amends. It also means being willing to work on yourself to prevent the same mistakes from happening again.

Patience: Rebuilding trust takes time, and it's essential to be patient. It's normal for your partner to have doubts and fears, and it may take a while for them to trust you again fully. It's essential to be patient and understanding, and not to pressure your partner into trusting you before they're ready.

Professional help: It can be helpful to seek professional help when rebuilding trust after infidelity. Couples therapy can provide a safe space to work through issues and learn new communication and coping skills. It can also provide a neutral third party to facilitate difficult conversations.

The significance of forgiveness in the process of healing

Forgiveness plays a critical role in the healing process after infidelity. It is a process of letting go of the anger, hurt, and resentment that comes with the betrayal and choosing to move forward in a positive way. Forgiveness does not mean forgetting or excusing the actions of the offending partner, but rather a decision to release the negative emotions associated with the betrayal.

Forgiveness can be a difficult process, and it may take time and effort to achieve. It requires a commitment to working through the pain and rebuilding trust with your partner. It is important to note that forgiveness is a personal decision and should not be rushed or forced.

To begin the process of forgiveness, it is important to acknowledge and express the emotions associated with the betrayal. This includes allowing yourself to feel anger, sadness and hurt. It may also involve communicating your feelings to your partner in a constructive way.

Forgiveness also requires the offending partner to take responsibility for their actions and show genuine remorse. This may involve offering a sincere apology, making amends, and taking concrete steps to rebuild trust in the relationship.

In addition, forgiveness requires a commitment to working through the healing process together as a couple. This may involve seeking the help of a therapist or counselor, developing healthy communication habits, and setting clear boundaries and expectations for the future.

Ultimately, forgiveness is a powerful tool for healing and rebuilding a relationship after infidelity. It requires courage, vulnerability, and a willingness to work through the pain together. With time, effort, and commitment, it is possible to move past the hurt and rebuild a stronger, more resilient relationship.

Chapter Seven

Creating New Patterns of Intimacy

Understanding the impact of the affair on your intimacy

Infidelity can have a significant impact on intimacy in a relationship. The breach of trust and betrayal can lead to feelings of hurt, anger, and resentment, which can make it difficult for partners to connect on an emotional and physical level. Understanding the impact of the affair on intimacy is an important step in rebuilding a healthy relationship.

After an affair, it is common for the injured partner to feel emotionally distant and disconnected from their partner. They may feel betrayed and struggle to trust their partner again. This can lead to a lack of emotional intimacy, which is critical for building a strong and healthy relationship. Emotional intimacy involves feeling secure and connected with your partner, being able to share your thoughts and feelings, and feeling supported and understood.

Infidelity can also have a significant impact on physical intimacy. The injured partner may feel angry and resentful and may find it difficult to be physically intimate with their partner. This can lead to a decrease in sexual desire and intimacy, which can further strain the relationship.

To rebuild intimacy after an affair, it is important to address the underlying issues that led to the infidelity in the first place. This may involve seeking the help of a therapist or counselor to work through the emotions associated with the affair and developing a plan to rebuild trust and connection in the relationship.

It is also important to communicate openly and honestly with your partner about your needs and desires and to be willing to listen and understand their perspective as well. This may involve taking things slowly and working together to rebuild trust and connection over time.

Rebuilding intimacy after an affair is not an easy process, and it may take time and effort to rebuild the emotional and physical connection in the relationship. However, with patience, commitment, and a willingness to work together, it is possible to rebuild a strong and healthy relationship.

Creating a new vision for your sexual relationship

After an affair, it's common for the couple's sexual relationship to be affected. The betrayed partner may experience a wide range of emotions, such as feeling hurt, angry, or uninterested in sex. Meanwhile, the unfaithful partner may feel guilt, shame, and a lack of desire to be intimate due to the emotional turmoil they are going through. However, it's important to acknowledge that it's possible to rebuild intimacy after infidelity. Here are some tips for creating a new vision for your sexual relationship:

Start with honest communication: To rebuild your sexual relationship, both partners need to be open and honest about their thoughts, feelings, and desires. It's essential to have frank conversations about what feels comfortable and what doesn't.

Take it slow: After infidelity, it's important to give yourself time to heal emotionally. Both partners may need time to rebuild trust and feel safe again. Therefore, taking it slow with physical intimacy can help both partners to ease back into the sexual relationship.

Try new things: After an affair, it's essential to create a new vision for your sexual relationship. This could involve trying new things, such as exploring each other's fantasies, experimenting with different positions, or incorporating toys or other tools into your sex life. However, it's crucial to do so in a way that feels safe and consensual for both partners.

Seek professional help: Sometimes, it may be helpful to seek the guidance of a professional therapist or sex therapist. They can provide a safe space to explore your thoughts and feelings about sex after infidelity and provide support as you navigate rebuilding your sexual relationship.

Practice patience and understanding: It's important to remember that rebuilding your sexual relationship after infidelity may take time. Both partners need to be patient and understanding with each other as they work to create a new vision for their intimacy. It's also essential to recognize that setbacks may occur along the way, and it's okay to ask for support when needed.

Building emotional intimacy through communication

When infidelity occurs in a relationship, it can have a significant impact on the couple's sexual intimacy. It is not uncommon for the hurt partner to feel a range of emotions, including anger, betrayal, and loss of desire. Additionally, the partner who committed the infidelity may feel guilt, shame, and anxiety, making it challenging to engage in sexual intimacy.

Developing a fresh perspective on sexual intimacy following a case of infidelity can feel like a challenging undertaking, but it is crucial for the recovery process. The following are some techniques that may assist:

Communicate openly and honestly: Both partners need to express their feelings and concerns about sexual intimacy. This requires creating a safe and non-judgmental space to have open and honest conversations.

Practice active listening: Listening is an essential skill when it comes to communication. Partners should listen to each other without interrupting, being defensive, or judging. Active listening can help improve communication and increase understanding.

Re-establish trust: Rebuilding trust takes time and effort. The partner who committed infidelity must demonstrate consistent behavior that promotes transparency, honesty, and accountability. This may include sharing their whereabouts, being open about their communication with others, and avoiding behavior that could trigger suspicion.

Focus on physical touch: Sometimes, sexual intimacy may be too challenging to engage in, but physical touch can help rebuild intimacy. Simple gestures like holding hands, hugging, or cuddling can help partners feel closer and more connected.

Experiment with new activities: Trying new activities or exploring new sexual experiences can help partners create new positive memories and associations with sexual intimacy. However, this should be done with mutual consent, respect, and communication.

Seek professional help: If rebuilding intimacy seems overwhelming or challenging, it may be beneficial to seek professional help from a therapist or counselor. A professional can help identify underlying issues, facilitate communication, and provide strategies to rebuild intimacy.

Chapter Eight

Moving Forward Together

Embracing a new vision for your relationship

After the discovery of an affair, it is common for both partners to feel lost and unsure about the future of their relationship. However, it is possible to rebuild trust, and intimacy, and create a new vision for your relationship.

First, it is important to acknowledge the pain and hurt caused by the affair and take responsibility for your actions. This means actively working to make amends for the pain caused and taking steps to ensure it does not happen again. It is also crucial to understand the complex emotions involved and be patient with the healing process.

Next, creating a safe and supportive environment for your partner is key. This means actively listening, empathizing, and validating your partner's experience. Encouraging open and honest communication can help build trust and allow both partners to express their emotions and needs.

It is also essential to embrace a new vision for your relationship. This means taking a fresh look at your priorities, values, and goals as a couple. Creating new rituals, traditions, and experiences can help build intimacy and strengthen your connection.

Additionally, rebuilding intimacy after an affair can be a challenge. It is essential to communicate openly about your needs and desires, take things slow, and seek support from a therapist if necessary. Both partners need to be willing to work together to create a new vision for their sexual relationship.

Ultimately, rebuilding a relationship after an affair requires patience, dedication, and a willingness to embrace change. It is possible to create a stronger, healthier, and more fulfilling relationship than before, but it takes effort from both partners.

Creating a shared future based on trust and respect

Creating a shared future based on trust and respect is an essential part of rebuilding a relationship after infidelity. It involves both partners working together to establish a new foundation for their relationship that is built on honesty, openness, and accountability.

The first step in creating a shared future is to acknowledge the past and the mistakes that were made. Both partners need to take responsibility for their actions and work to understand the impact that the affair had on their relationship. This can involve seeking therapy or counseling to help process emotions and establish healthy communication patterns.

Once the past has been acknowledged, it's important to establish clear boundaries and expectations for the future. This may involve setting ground rules for communication, establishing trust-building exercises, or creating a shared vision for the relationship that aligns with both partners' values and needs.

Creating a shared future also involves practicing ongoing transparency and accountability. Both partners need to be committed to being open and honest with each other, sharing their thoughts and feelings without fear of judgment or retaliation. This can involve setting up regular check-ins, such as weekly or monthly meetings, to discuss any concerns or issues that arise.

Additionally, it's important to prioritize intimacy and connection in the relationship. This may involve exploring new ways to connect with each other, such as through shared activities or hobbies, or taking steps to improve sexual intimacy. It's important to approach intimacy with openness and patience, understanding that it may take time to fully rebuild this aspect of the relationship.

Ultimately, creating a shared future based on trust and respect requires both partners to be committed to the process of rebuilding their relationship. It may involve setbacks and challenges along the way, but with a shared commitment to honesty, openness, and communication, it's possible to establish a strong and healthy foundation for the future.

Celebrating your progress and committing to continued growth

Recovering from infidelity is a challenging journey, and it's essential to celebrate the progress you've made along the way. This helps to acknowledge the effort and hard work that both partners have put in to rebuild the relationship.

It's important to take time to recognize and appreciate the milestones you've reached. These could be small victories like having an open and honest conversation without getting defensive or more significant accomplishments like establishing a new foundation of trust.

Celebrating progress can help to boost motivation and reinforce the commitment to continue working towards a healthy, fulfilling relationship. It's a way to acknowledge the effort and progress you've made while also setting your sights on what's to come.

Partners can celebrate progress by recognizing and expressing gratitude for each other's efforts, planning special activities to mark significant milestones, or reflecting on the progress made in therapy sessions.

At the same time, it's crucial to commit to continued growth and improvement. Building a healthy, fulfilling relationship takes ongoing effort, and it's important to stay committed to the journey. This might involve continuing therapy sessions or seeking out additional resources, such as self-help books or couples retreats.

Partners can commit to continued growth by setting new goals and aspirations for their relationship, continuing to prioritize open and honest communication, and being open to feedback and growth opportunities.

Ultimately, celebrating progress and committing to continued growth helps to create a shared vision for the future. This vision is based on trust, respect, and a shared commitment to building a healthy, fulfilling relationship.

Chapter Nine

Common Pitfalls and How to Avoid Them

The most common mistakes after infidelity

Infidelity is a significant breach of trust in a relationship that can leave both partners feeling hurt, betrayed, and unsure of the future of their relationship. While healing and rebuilding trust after infidelity is possible, there are some common mistakes that people make that can hinder the process. Here are some of the most common mistakes after infidelity:

Minimizing or denying the impact of the affair: It can be tempting to downplay the severity of the affair or pretend that it didn't happen at all.

However, this can leave the hurt partner feeling invalidated and dismissed.

Blaming the hurt partner: It is not uncommon for the unfaithful partner to try to shift the blame onto their partner for their infidelity. This is not only unfair but also prevents true accountability and healing from taking place.

Rushing the healing process: Healing after infidelity takes time and cannot be rushed. Trying to move past the affair too quickly or without proper communication and support can lead to further damage.

Failing to take responsibility for actions: The unfaithful partner must take responsibility for their actions and the pain they have caused. Without accepting responsibility, there can be no real healing or progress.

Not addressing underlying issues: Infidelity is often a symptom of deeper issues within the relationship, such as communication problems or unmet needs. Failing to address these issues can leave the relationship vulnerable to future infidelity.

Not seeking professional help: Healing from infidelity is challenging, and seeking professional help from a therapist or counselor can provide much-needed support and guidance.

Not being consistent: Rebuilding trust requires consistent effort over time. Failing to follow through on commitments or promises can make the hurt partner feel even more mistrustful and hurt.

Neglecting self-care: Both partners must take care of their own emotional and physical needs during the healing process. Neglecting self-care can lead to further emotional distress and damage to the relationship.

Strategies to avoid falling back into old patterns

Infidelity can have a devastating impact on a relationship, and one of the biggest challenges in the healing process is avoiding falling back into old patterns that led to the affair. Here are some strategies to help avoid making the same mistakes:

Be honest with yourself: The first step in avoiding old patterns is to recognize them. Take a close look at your behaviors, attitudes, and beliefs that contributed to the affair. This requires taking an honest and introspective look at yourself and your relationship.

Take responsibility: Owning your role in the affair is crucial to avoid falling back into old patterns. Acknowledge your mistakes, take responsibility for your actions, and commit to making changes.

Set clear boundaries: Establishing clear boundaries can help prevent slipping into old patterns. This may include avoiding certain situations or behaviors that were problematic in the past.

Promote transparent and sincere communication: Effective communication plays a crucial role in every relationship, particularly following an act of infidelity. Each partner must be ready to express their emotions, requirements, and aspirations candidly and transparently.

Seek professional help: It can be helpful to seek professional counseling or therapy to work through the aftermath of infidelity and to develop strategies to avoid falling back into old patterns. A trained therapist can help you identify your triggers, develop healthy coping mechanisms, and establish effective communication strategies.

Focus on the present and future: While it's important to acknowledge and learn from past mistakes, it's also important to focus on the present and future. Let go of the past and work together to create a new vision for your relationship based on trust, respect, and mutual support.

Prioritize self-nurturing: Nurturing yourself is vital for the process of recovery. Engage in activities that foster both physical and emotional well-being, such as working out, practicing mindfulness, or spending quality time with cherished individuals.

When you feel content with yourself, it can be simpler to bring positive transformations to your relationship.

Maintaining your commitment to healing

Healing after infidelity is a challenging journey that requires dedication and commitment from both partners. While it may be difficult at times, it is crucial to maintain your commitment to the healing process to rebuild trust, repair the relationship, and move forward together. Here are some strategies for maintaining your commitment to healing:

Continuously work on communication: Open and honest communication is key to maintaining a healthy relationship. Make a conscious effort to communicate regularly, clearly, and respectfully with your partner. Be willing to listen to their perspective and feelings without becoming defensive.

Keep your promises: Consistency and reliability are essential in rebuilding trust. Follow through on your commitments and promises, no matter how small they may seem.

Cultivate empathy and comprehension: Endeavor to view the situation from your partner's point of view and try to comprehend their perspective. Display kindness and endurance as they navigate through their emotions and sentiments.

Avoid blame and defensiveness: Taking responsibility for your actions and avoiding blame is crucial in rebuilding trust. Avoid being defensive or making excuses for your behavior, and instead, take ownership of your mistakes.

Seek professional help: Healing after infidelity can be challenging, and it may be helpful to seek professional help from a therapist or counselor. A professional can provide guidance, support, and tools to help you navigate the healing process.

Prioritize self-care: Healing after infidelity is emotionally taxing, and it is essential to take care of yourself physically and emotionally. Make time for self-care activities that help you relax, de-stress, and refocus.

Celebrate progress: Celebrate the small victories along the way and acknowledge the progress you and your partner have made. This can help you stay motivated and committed to the healing process.

Chapter Ten

Seeking Professional Help

When to seek professional help

When dealing with the aftermath of infidelity, it is important to acknowledge that healing is a journey and it may not always be easy to navigate. Seeking professional help may be necessary to help both partners navigate the emotional complexities involved and find a way forward.

Here are some situations where seeking professional help may be beneficial:

Lack of progress: If you and your partner have been working on healing after infidelity, but you still find yourself stuck in old patterns or unable to move forward, it may be time to seek professional help.

Difficulty communicating: If you and your partner struggle to communicate effectively or have trouble discussing your emotions or experiences, a therapist or counselor can help facilitate healthy communication and guide you toward solutions.

Unresolved trauma: Infidelity can be traumatic for both partners, and it may trigger past traumas or unresolved issues. A therapist or counselor can help you work through these issues and prevent them from interfering with your healing process.

Trust issues: Rebuilding trust after infidelity can be challenging and may require professional guidance. A therapist can help you identify the root of your trust issues and provide tools to help you and your partner rebuild trust.

Individual issues: Infidelity can also bring up individual issues, such as anxiety or depression, that may require individual therapy to address.

Concerns for safety: If the infidelity involved emotional or physical abuse, it may be necessary to seek professional help to ensure the safety of both partners.

Overall, seeking professional help is a sign of strength and a commitment to healing. It is important to find a therapist or counselor who specializes in infidelity and has experience working with couples. Remember, healing takes time, effort, and patience, but with the right support, you and your partner can move forward and build a stronger, healthier relationship.

The benefits of couples counseling

Couples counseling can be incredibly beneficial for couples who are dealing with the aftermath of infidelity. Here are some of the key benefits:

Improved Communication: One of the primary benefits of couples counseling is improved communication. Counselors can help couples to learn how to communicate more effectively and express their needs and concerns in a healthy way.

This can help to prevent misunderstandings and conflicts and can create a stronger, more supportive relationship.

Rebuilding Trust: Rebuilding trust is a critical component of healing after infidelity. Couples counseling can provide a safe space for couples to work on rebuilding trust and intimacy and can help to establish new patterns of behavior that foster trust and honesty.

Identifying Underlying Issues: Infidelity is often a symptom of deeper issues within a relationship. Couples counseling can help to identify these underlying issues, such as communication problems or unresolved conflicts, and can provide strategies for addressing them.

Providing a Neutral Space: Infidelity can create a lot of emotional turmoil, and it can be difficult for couples to work through these issues on their own. Couples counseling provides a neutral space where both partners can feel heard and understood, and where they can work through their issues with the guidance of a trained professional.

Offering Emotional Support: Dealing with the aftermath of infidelity can be incredibly difficult, and it can be helpful to have emotional support during this time. Couples counseling can provide a supportive environment where both partners can feel heard and validated, and where they can work through their emotions in a healthy way.

Learning New Coping Strategies: Coping with the aftermath of infidelity can be challenging, and couples counseling can provide new coping strategies for dealing with the emotional fallout. This can include strategies for managing anger, coping with feelings of betrayal, and rebuilding self-esteem.

Finding a qualified therapist

Finding a qualified therapist can be a crucial step in the healing process after infidelity. Here are some tips for finding a qualified therapist:

Look for licensed professionals: A licensed therapist has the education, training, and experience required to help you and your partner navigate the challenges of infidelity.

Seek out a therapist with experience in couples counseling: A therapist with experience in couples counseling can help you and your partner work through the challenges of infidelity and develop a plan for rebuilding your relationship.

Check credentials and references: Look for a therapist who has the appropriate credentials and has received positive feedback from previous clients. You can check their credentials with professional organizations or state licensing boards.

Consider the therapist's approach: Different therapists use different approaches to therapy. Make sure the therapist's approach aligns with your needs and preferences.

Schedule a consultation: Before committing to a therapist, schedule a consultation to discuss your needs and concerns. This will give you an opportunity to see if the therapist is a good fit for you and your partner.

Look for a therapist who is non-judgmental and empathetic: A therapist who is non-judgmental and empathetic can help create a safe space for you and your partner to explore the complex emotions and challenges that come with infidelity.

Consider logistics: Look for a therapist who is conveniently located and has availability that fits your schedule.

Healing from affairs 102

Conclusion

The power of healing and forgiveness

Healing and forgiveness can be incredibly powerful forces in the aftermath of infidelity. While the journey to healing can be difficult and complex, it is possible to emerge from the experience with a deeper sense of understanding and a stronger relationship.

Healing begins with acknowledging the pain and hurt caused by the affair and taking responsibility for one's actions. This includes being open and honest about the affair, listening actively to one's partner's feelings, and showing empathy and understanding. It also means being patient and allowing one's partner to process their emotions in their own time, and not rushing the healing process.

Forgiveness can be a transformative process that allows couples to move forward and create a new vision for their relationship. However, forgiveness is not something that can be forced or demanded, and it can take time and effort to achieve. It involves letting go of anger and resentment and choosing to focus on the positive aspects of the relationship.

Forgiveness is not the same as forgetting or excusing the behavior that caused the pain. It is important to remember that forgiveness does not mean that the hurt and betrayal never occurred, but rather that it is possible to move beyond the pain and rebuild trust and intimacy in the relationship.

It is also important to recognize that healing and forgiveness are ongoing processes. Even after progress has been made, it is possible to experience setbacks or triggers that can cause old wounds to resurface. This is why it is important to maintain a commitment to healing and to seek professional help if needed.

Ultimately, the power of healing and forgiveness lies in the ability to create a new future for the relationship. By working together to overcome the pain and betrayal of infidelity, couples can emerge stronger and more resilient than ever before.

Moving forward with hope and optimism

Moving forward after infidelity can be a challenging journey, but it's possible to do so with hope and optimism. Here are some key factors to consider:

Acceptance: Acceptance of what happened is an important first step towards healing. This includes accepting the reality of the affair, accepting responsibility for your actions, and accepting the pain that has been caused.

Forgiveness: Forgiveness can be a powerful tool for moving forward. This doesn't mean forgetting what happened, but rather acknowledging the hurt and choosing to let go of the anger and resentment. Forgiveness can bring a sense of peace and closure.

Communication: Open and honest communication is vital to moving forward. This includes sharing your thoughts and feelings with your partner, actively listening to their perspective, and being willing to make changes to improve the relationship.

Commitment: Rebuilding a relationship after infidelity requires a strong commitment from both partners. This means being willing to put in the time and effort to rebuild trust and being patient with each other throughout the healing process.

Growth: Healing from infidelity can be an opportunity for personal and relationship growth. It can lead to a deeper understanding of each other, increased empathy and compassion, and a stronger connection.

Support: Seeking support from a therapist, support group, or trusted friends and family members can be helpful in the healing process. It's important to find people who are non-judgmental, supportive, and understanding.

Moving forward with hope and optimism after infidelity is possible, but it requires a willingness to be vulnerable, communicate openly, and commit to the healing process. By taking these steps, couples can rebuild their relationship and create a stronger, more fulfilling future together.

Embracing the opportunity for growth and renewal

Infidelity can be an incredibly painful experience, but it can also be an opportunity for growth and renewal. Both partners have the potential to emerge from the experience stronger, more self-aware, and more committed to each other than ever before.

The first step in this process is acknowledging the pain and hurt caused by the affair. This involves taking responsibility for one's actions and actively seeking to make amends for the pain caused. It is important to understand the reasons behind the affair, to take ownership of one's actions, and to make things right.

Creating a safe and supportive environment for the hurt partner is crucial. This involves active listening, empathizing with their feelings, and validating their experience. It is important to encourage open and honest communication, while also being patient and allowing them to process their emotions.

Rebuilding trust is essential to moving forward in the relationship. This can be achieved through transparency and accountability, as well as a commitment to creating a shared future based on trust and respect. Couples counseling can also be incredibly beneficial in this process, providing a safe and neutral space to work through issues and develop a plan for moving forward.

It is important to avoid falling back into old patterns and to maintain a commitment to healing. This may involve developing coping strategies for both partners, navigating difficult conversations and triggers, and celebrating progress while committing to continued growth.

The power of healing and forgiveness cannot be overstated. While the journey may be difficult, it is possible to move forward with hope and optimism, embracing the opportunity for growth and renewal. It is possible to emerge from the experience stronger, more resilient, and more committed to each other than ever before.

Bonus: MOOD TRACKER

A mood tracker is a tool that allows you to record and monitor your moods and emotions over time. By regularly tracking your moods, you can start to identify patterns and triggers that affect your emotional state.

How mood tracker can help in the healing process of infidelity

Identify triggers: Infidelity can trigger a range of emotions, from anger and sadness to anxiety and depression. By tracking your moods, you can start to identify what triggers these emotions and work on avoiding or managing those triggers.

Monitor progress: Healing from infidelity is a gradual process, and it's important to recognize and celebrate progress along the way. A mood tracker can help you track your progress and see how your emotional state is changing over time.

Communicate with your partner: If you're working through the aftermath of infidelity with your partner, a mood tracker can be a helpful tool for communicating about your emotional state. By sharing your mood tracker with your partner, you can help them understand how you're feeling and what triggers your emotions.

Seek professional help: If you're struggling to manage your emotions and work through the aftermath of infidelity on your own, a mood tracker can be a useful tool to share with a therapist or counselor. They can use the data you've collected to help you develop coping strategies and monitor progress over time.

Overall, a mood tracker can be a powerful tool for anyone working through the aftermath of infidelity. It can help you identify triggers, monitor progress, communicate with your partner, and seek professional help when needed.

S/N	Emotion	What happened?
1		
2		
3		
4		
5		
6		
7		

8		
9		
10		
11		
12		
13		
14		
15		
16		

17		
18		
19		
20		
21		

Dear Reader,

Thank you for choosing to read my book, HOW TO HELP YOUR WIFE HEAL FROM YOUR AFFAIR. I hope you found it informative and helpful.

If you have a moment, I would greatly appreciate it if you could leave a review on Amazon. Your feedback would help me better understand what readers appreciate about my work, and would also provide valuable information to potential readers.

Your honest review would be greatly appreciated, and would help me continue to improve as a writer. I truly value your opinion, and I thank you in advance for taking the time to share your thoughts.

Thank you again for choosing to read my book, and for considering leaving a review.

Best regards,

Steve Collins

Printed in Great Britain
by Amazon

32082236R00066